Greetings from Ocean City, Maryland

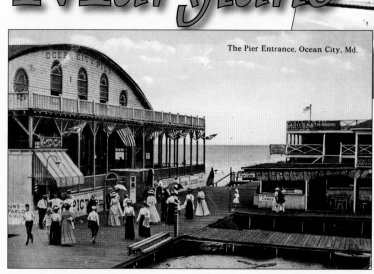

17—Boardwalk and Beach Looking North, Ocean City, Md.

3B-H1359

The Pier Entrance, Ocean City, Md.

Mary L. Martin and
Nathaniel Wolfgang-Price

Schiffer ®
Publishing Ltd

4880 Lower Valley Road   Atglen, Pennsylvania 19310

Acknowledgments

Many thanks go to Josh Stabler for his work with the captions and for helping to get this project started.

Published by Schiffer Publishing Ltd.
4880 Lower Valley Road
Atglen, PA 19310
Phone: (610) 593-1777; Fax: (610) 593-2002
E-mail: Info@schifferbooks.com

For the largest selection of fine reference books on this and related subjects, please visit our web site at **www.schifferbooks.com**
We are always looking for people to write books on new and related subjects. If you have an idea for a book please contact us at the above address.

This book may be purchased from the publisher.
Include $3.95 for shipping.
Please try your bookstore first.
You may write for a free catalog.

In Europe, Schiffer books are distributed by
Bushwood Books
6 Marksbury Ave.
Kew Gardens
Surrey TW9 4JF England
Phone: 44 (0) 20 8392-8585; Fax: 44 (0) 20 8392-9876
E-mail: info@bushwoodbooks.co.uk
Website: www.bushwoodbooks.co.uk
Free postage in the U.K., Europe; air mail at cost.

Designed by Mark David Bowyer
Type set in Geometric231 Hv BT / Aldine721 BT
ISBN: 978-0-7643-2656-1
Printed in China

Contents

Preface

Historic Images Through Postcards

Postcards are said to be the most popular collectible history has ever known. The urge to horde them sprang up with the birth of this means of communication at the turn of the twentieth century, and has endured great changes in the printing industry. Today, postcard shows take place every weekend somewhere in the country, or the world, and millions of pieces of ephemera lie in wait for those who collect obscure topics or town views.

Postcards once served as the email of their day. Beginning in the 1890s, they were the fastest, most popular means of communication in the United States. These timely cards provided a way to send scenes through the mail, along with brief messages–a way to enchant friends and family with the places travelers visited, to send local scenes, or to share favorite topics of imagery. They even provided the latest breaking news, as images of fires, floods, shipwrecks, and festivals were often available in postcard form within hours of an event. Moreover, mail delivery was received by most homes in the United States at least twice a day. So someone might send a morning postcard inviting a friend to dinner that evening, and receive an RSVP in time to shop for food.

The messages shared and the beautiful scenes combine to create the timeless appeal of postcards as a collectible. Most importantly, history is recorded by the pictures of the times, moments in time reflecting an alluring past.

Dating Postcards

Determining the ages of postcards, because of the specifics of the times, is not terribly difficult.

Pioneer Era (1893-1898): Most pioneer cards in today's collections begin with cards placed on sale at the Columbian Exposition in Chicago on May 1, 1893. These were illustrations on government printed postal cards and privately printed souvenir cards. The government cards had the printed one-cent stamp, while souvenir cards required a two-cent adhesive postage stamp to be applied. Writing was not permitted on the address side of the card.

Private Mailing Card Era (1898-1901): On May 19, 1898, private printers were granted permission, by an act of Congress, to print and sell cards that bore the inscription "Private Mailing Card." A one-cent adhesive stamp was required. A dozen or more American printers began to take postcards seriously. Writing was still not permitted on the back.

Post Card Era - Undivided Back (1901-1907): New U.S. postal regulations on December 24, 1901, stipulated that the words "Post Card" should be printed at the top of the address side of privately printed cards. Government-issued cards were to be designated as "Postal Cards." Writing was still not permitted on the address side. In this era, private citizens began to take black and white photographs and have them printed on paper with post card backs.

Example of a postcard with an undivided back. Senders could only write the address on this side of the card. Any message needed to be written on the front of the card along with the picture.

Early Divided Back Era (1907-1914): Postcards with a divided back were permitted in Britain in 1902, but not in the U.S. until March 1, 1907. The address was to be written on the right side; the left side was for writing messages. Many millions of cards were published in this era. Up to this point, most postcards were printed in Germany, which was far ahead of the United States in the use of lithographic processes. With the advent of World War I, the suppliers of postcards for American consumption switched from Germany to England and the United States.

White Border Era (1915-1930): Most United States postcards were printed during this period. To save ink, publishers left a clear border around the view, thus these postcards are referred to as "White Border" cards. The relatively high cost of labor, along with inexperience and changes in public taste, resulted in the production of poor quality cards during this period. Furthermore, strong competition in a narrowing market caused many publishers to go out of business.

Linen Era (1930-1944): New printing processes allowed printing on postcards with high rag content that created a textured finish. These cheap cards allowed the use of gaudy dyes for coloring.

Photochrome Era (1945 to date): "Chrome" postcards began to dominate the scene soon after the Union Oil Company placed them in its western service stations in 1939. Mike Roberts pioneered with his "WESCO" cards soon after World War II. Three-dimensional postcards also appeared in this era.

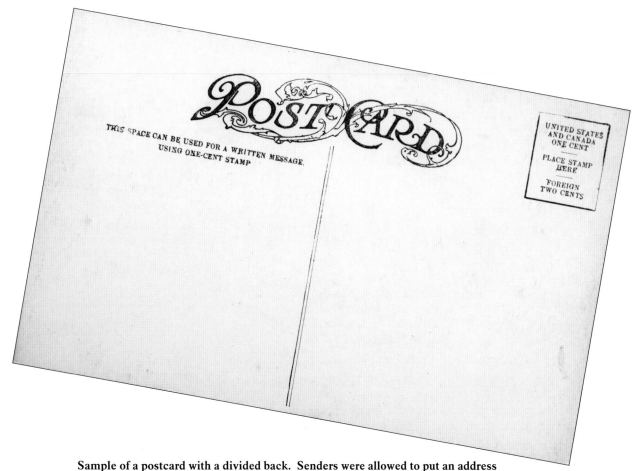

Sample of a postcard with a divided back. Senders were allowed to put an address on the right hand side of the postcard and a message on the left side.

Concerning Ocean City

Introduction

On July 4, 1875, 800 people from the mid-Atlantic states converged on Ocean City, Maryland, to celebrate the grand opening of the Atlantic Hotel, an event which marked the birth of what would become a world-class seaside resort. One hotel soon became dozens, as investors and developers purchased lots for building summer cottages, rooming houses, hotels, stores, and restaurants. Today, Ocean City, Maryland, stretches from the Ocean City Inlet north to the Delaware state line, occupying a space filled with 500 rental apartment buildings of varying sizes, 81 motels, 38 hotels, and an 1,800-lot mobile home park. Throughout this area are scattered 158 restaurants, 70 real estate and rental agencies, and 66 amusement parks, waterslides, arcades, and miniature golf courses.

Even when it was little more than a remote collection of cottages and rooming houses in the middle of nowhere on the Delmarva Peninsula, Ocean City had something for everyone. For the sportsman there were shorebirds to hunt and fish to catch. For the boater there were the spacious waters of the Atlantic Ocean and Sinepuxent Bay. For the socialite there were fine dinners at the Atlantic, the Plimhimmon, and the Harrison Hall Hotels. There were amusements and games on the boardwalk, concerts and dances on the pier, and plenty to do on the beach. No matter what their tastes in activities were, and no matter their reasons – whether it was for sport, pleasure, or to simply to "get away from it all" – visitors were always welcome in Ocean City.

Far more convenient, and in many cases, easier to use than a telephone or a telegraph, the postcard remained one of the best ways for these visitors to communicate. They were just the right size to slip into a suitcase to take home as souvenirs or to jot down a quick message to friends and family letting them know that the sender had arrived safely, missed them, and was having a good time. These postcards also acted as a form of advertising, showcasing the city's best features and encouraging the recipients to visit this place and see these features for themselves.

In this book, hand-tinted and black and white postcards from the 1900s to the 1990s showcase some of Ocean City, Maryland's best features. Quoted material from the back of the cards and excerpts from the messages written on them, along with historical trivia is included with the captions. This text helps to paint an interesting and enjoyable picture of Ocean City's past and present.

Greetings from Ocean City Maryland, "The White Marlin Capital of the World."

Cancelled 1908, $24-26

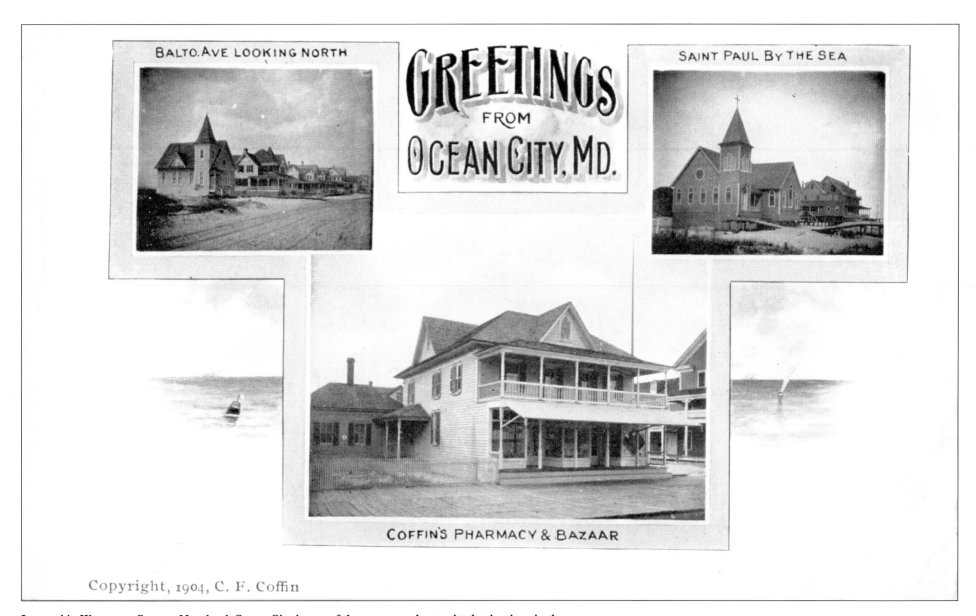

BALTO. AVE LOOKING NORTH

GREETINGS FROM OCEAN CITY, MD.

SAINT PAUL BY THE SEA

COFFIN'S PHARMACY & BAZAAR

Copyright, 1904, C. F. Coffin

Located in Worcester County, Maryland, Ocean City is one of the most popular tourist destinations in the Mid-Atlantic region.

Circa 1900s, $30

More "Greetings from Ocean City, Maryland."

Cancelled 1954, $7-9

"A Great Big Hello" from Ocean City.

Circa 1980, $3-5

History

In 1868 Colonel Lemeul Showell, a prosperous landowner from Worcester County, Maryland, came together with several of his friends and business associates to organize the Atlantic Hotel Company. Showell had built a summer cottage on the future site of Ocean City and believed the land had potential for future development.

In 1874 the Wicomico and Pocomoke Railroad extended their line to the mainland shore of Sinepuxent Bay, which in turn linked the area with Wilmington, Delaware; Philadelphia, Pennsylvania; and other points north. Seeing possibilities that lay ahead, members of the Atlantic Hotel Company quickly arranged a meeting with Stephen Taber, a land speculator who owned much of the land the Company planned to develop. Tabor agreed to let them have a ten-acre site of their choice to build a hotel, plus an additional fifty acres for a town if the hotel was built.

The Atlantic Hotel Company sprang into action and construction began on the hotel. The project proceeded smoothly and in 1875, the Atlantic Hotel opened on July 4. That date also marks the founding of the town of Ocean City itself. On July 28, 1876 Stephen Taber made his promise good and deeded fifty acres to the Atlantic Hotel Company. Thus, Ocean City, Maryland, was born.

The name for the proposed resort, "Ocean City," came from a meeting of the stockholders of the Atlantic Hotel Company held in Salisbury, Maryland. Of the various names suggested, which included "Sinepuxent City," "Beach City," and "Ladies Resort to the Ocean," "Ocean City" was most popular and became the name for the new community.

Development in Ocean City continued at a brisk pace. Many investors and private individuals purchased plots of land in order to build hotels, rooming houses, summer cottages, and other businesses essential to the operation of a seaside resort. In 1892 the Sinepuxent Beach Company purchased the Atlantic Hotel and 1,600 acres on both sides of original plots, planning two subdivisions, further increasing the area of the town and opening it up for additional development.

Another milestone in Ocean City's development occurred when the city was hit by a hurricane in 1933. The storm caused between $350,000 to $500,000 worth of damage and carved an inlet across the southern tip of the city, separating it from Assateague Island. Seeing possible benefit this new inlet could have for the city, the inlet was made permanent. This gave ships docking on the bay side of the city, created an easy path to the ocean, and helped to make Ocean City one of the country's best fishing ports.

Much of the modern development of Ocean City did not take place until after World War II, when the Chesapeake Bay Bridge opened, making the city easily accessible to people living in the Baltimore-Washington corridor. This area between Baltimore, Maryland, and Washington, D.C., includes Anne Arundel, Howard, Montgomery, and Prince George Counties. The bridge and opening of the Chesapeake Bay Bridge-Tunnel in 1964 enabled more visitors to come, and that in turn created the need for more development. In the 1970s, over 10,000 condominium units were built, peppering the city's skyline with high-rise buildings.

Today, Ocean City is one of the largest vacation areas on the East Coast, extending nearly eleven miles from the edge of the inlet to the Maryland-Delaware state line. The city is home to a year-round population of 8,000, most of whom work for the city, and a season population of well over 100,000.

From the Back: Sinepuxent Bay is on the left the Atlantic Ocean is on the right. These aerial views of Ocean City, Maryland, show the beautiful motels of the northern section."

Circa 1980s, $5-7

The city itself is home to over five hundred rental apartment buildings, thirty-eight hotels, eighty-one motels, 158 restaurants, and sixty-six amusement parks, arcades, waterslides, and miniature golf-courses.

Circa 1960s, $6-8

An aerial view of Ocean City showing Sinepuxent Bay and Philadelphia and St. Louis Avenues.

Cancelled 1966, $5-8

Ocean City is visited by so many tourists annually that during the summer months it is Maryland's second largest city.

Circa 1960s, $4-6

Ocean City is located on the Delmarva Peninsula, a peninsula on the East Coast divided between Maryland, Virginia, and Delaware.

Circa 1940s, $7-9

Another aerial view of Ocean City, Maryland.

Circa 1940s, $5-7

At present, Ocean City is nearly eleven miles long but is only four and a half blocks wide.

Circa 1970s, $4-6

A bird's-eye-view of Ocean City, as
seen from the Atlantic Ocean.

Circa 1970s, $3-5

An aerial view showing some of the high-rise hotels and rental
apartment buildings located along the beach.

Circa 1990s, $3-5

More of Ocean City's distinctive beach front high-rises.

Circa 1990s, $3-5

An aerial view of the Heliport and Ship Café Island.

Circa 1960s, $4-6

Bird's-eye-view of Ocean City, showing The Fishing Pier and part of The Boardwalk.

Circa 1980s, $2-4

From the back: "The beauty of Ocean City at night can be seen in this photo looking south from 94th St. along the coastal highway from the top of the beautiful 9400 condominium."

Cancelled 1978, $2-4

Inside Ocean City

Public Buildings and Streets

A plan drawn up by members of the Atlantic Hotel Company, dated August 31, 1875, reveals the early layout of Ocean City, consisting of 205 building lots spread over a fifty-acre plot of land. The plan called for four avenues (St. Louis, Philadelphia, Baltimore, and Atlantic) running north to south and seven streets (Caroline, Talbot, Dorchester, Somerset, Wicomico, Worchester, and South Division) running east to west. Additional development by the Sinepuxent Beach Company saw the laying of new streets and avenues to the north and the south of the original plan. Following the plan, the north-south avenues were named and the east-west streets were numbered. The northern development began at North Division Street and extended north to 33rd Street. From the south the new streets began at

South Division Street and ran to South 10th Street on Assateague Island. Much of the southern development was lost during the 1933 hurricane or is now part of the Assateague National Seashore; only South 1st and South 2nd Streets remain. As Ocean City has expanded north, east, and west, new streets and avenues have been laid out with the east to west streets being numbered extending north to 146th Street and the north to south avenues being named.

While it is was first and foremost a resort community, Ocean City was still a community and had need for the basic public institutions that every community needs to function, such as schools, a post office, and a city hall. Ocean City's current City Hall was built in 1915 for use as an elementary and high school, and was purchased by the Town of Ocean City in 1968.

The present City Hall, built by the State of Maryland on Baltimore Avenue, was finished on June 30, 1915. It was used as an elementary and high school until 1965, when the elementary students were moved to a school in West Ocean City. The building was purchased by the Town on Ocean City in 1968 for use as the city hall.

Circa 1970s, $3-5

From the back: "Con. Hall was formally dedicated and open for use on April 18, 1970. The Hall is available for conventions, concerts, dances and trade shows. This building has a unique design suitable for all events."

Circa 1970s, $4-6

Convention Hall - Ocean City, Maryland

Photo by Richard C. Pulling

The Roland E. Powell Convention Center was built by the state of Maryland to further stimulate tourism and encourage year-round activity in Ocean City.

Circa 1970s, $3-5

15

BALTIMORE AVENUE, SHOWING AUTO LINE, OCEAN CITY, MD.

Baltimore Avenue was one of four north-south facing avenues that were part of Ocean City's original development plan.

Circa 1920s, $4-6

Churches

In 1897 a map of Ocean City was laid out showing the lay out of the Boardwalk along with the locations of the city's various hotels and rooming houses. Among those were four small churches – Catholic, Episcopal, Methodist, and Presbyterian. All four were too small to support a full-time pastor and relied on visiting ministers and lay preachers to conduct services.

The first church built in Ocean City was St. Mary's Star of the Sea Catholic Church built in 1878 by Thomas A. Becker, Bishop of the See of Wilmington. Ironically, the only Catholics in Ocean City at the time of the Church's construction were vacationers, the Catholic population did not begin to grow until the year-round population did. After St. Mary's other churches St. Paul's By-the-Sea (Episcopal), Atlantic United Methodist, and First Presbyterian were established. Like St. Mary's, their congregations were made primarily made up of vacationers but grew in membership once a year-round population became established. Today, Ocean City Maryland is home to large number of churches and other religious institutions and are well attended by vacationers and year-round residents alike.

First Presbyterian Church, Ocean City, Md.

The original First Presbyterian Church building was built on a lot on Baltimore Avenue donated by Alice Waggaman, one of the investors in the Sinepuxent Beach Company. Members of the church raised money for the new church building by selling homemade candy and flowers on The Boardwalk.

Circa 1920s, $4-6

First Presbyterian Church at its present location on Philadelphia Ave. at 13ᵗʰ Street.

Circa 1970s, $4-6

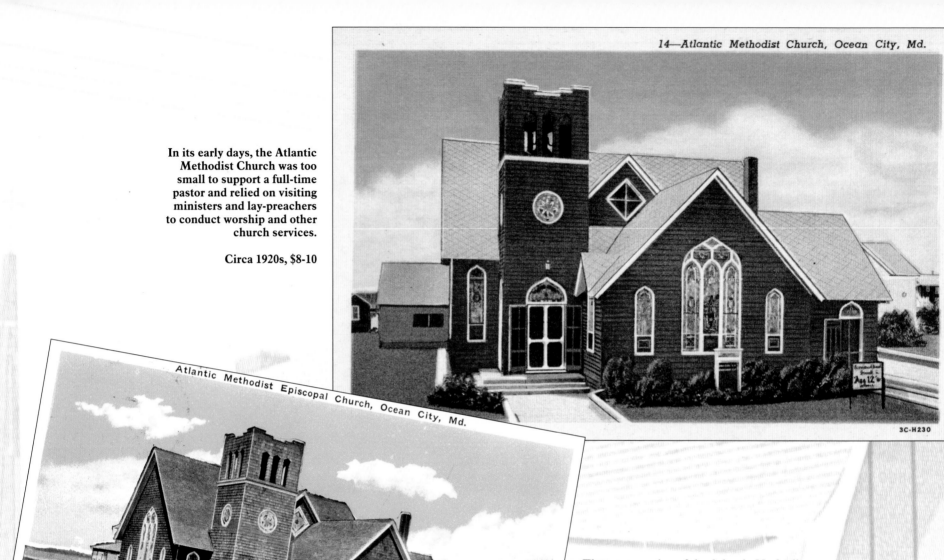

14—Atlantic Methodist Church, Ocean City, Md.

In its early days, the Atlantic Methodist Church was too small to support a full-time pastor and relied on visiting ministers and lay-preachers to conduct worship and other church services.

Circa 1920s, $8-10

3C-H230

Atlantic Methodist Episcopal Church, Ocean City, Md.

The congregation of the Atlantic Methodist Church met in a number of locations throughout the Ocean City before building a church building in 1919.

Cancelled 1938, $9-11

10—Holy Savior Catholic Church, Ocean City, Md.

3C-H1297

Holy Savior Catholic Church, one of the three Catholic churches located in Ocean City.

Circa 1940s, $5-7

The new church building for the Atlantic Methodist Church was built on the corner of Baltimore Avenue and 4th Street in 1962.

Circa 1960s, $4-6

19

Many of the Catholics who came to Ocean City during the resort's early days, came as visitors during the summer.

Circa 1960s, $4-6

Built in 1878, St. Mary's Star of the Sea Catholic Church was the first church built in Ocean City.

Cancelled 1933, $14-16

St. Mary's Star of the Sea Catholic Church, Ocean City, Md.

37282

St. Mary's Star of the Sea was built Thomas A. Becker, the Bishop of Diocese of Wilmington. The bishop would often spend the summer months in Ocean City and would bring all the priests in his diocese to the city for a spiritual retreat once a year.

Circa 1970s, $4-6

ST. PAUL'S EPISCOPAL CHURCH, OCEAN CITY, MD.

St. Paul's By-the-Sea Episcopal Church was first organized in 1880 and met in a small building near the Congress Hall Hotel.

Circa 1920s, $11-13

Sometime around the turn of the century, St. Paul's sold its first building and used the proceeds from the sale to build its present building at 3rd Street and Baltimore Avenue.

Circa 1960s, $3-5

21

Bridges

Located on an island, the area that would become Ocean City seemed ideal for a resort community, being cut off from the mainland of the Delmarva Peninsula by Sinepuxent Bay. This also meant, however, that a visitor had to cross the bay to get to the resort. In the early days, visitors were ferried to Ocean City by boat. When Ocean City began to grow as a resort, a more efficient way across Sinepuxent Bay was developed.

In 1876 the Wicomico and Pocomoke Railroad built a trestle bridge from the Delmarva Peninsula to Ocean City, running the track from the Peninsula and across the bay to a depot at Wicomico Street. Also designed to accommodate foot and wagon traffic, the railroad bridge was the only bridge across the bay and the only way, besides taking a boat, to get to Ocean City from the mainland until 1916.

In 1916, another bridge designed for automobile traffic was built by the State of Maryland. The automobile bridge was eventually replaced with the U.S. Route 50 Bridge, now known as the Henry Kelley Memorial Bridge, named after one of Ocean City's most memorable mayors. Another automobile bridge, the Maryland Route 90 Bridge, was built in 1967 to help alleviate some of the traffic backup caused by the large number of drivers trying to get into Ocean City.

While the bridges have helped ease traffic flow to and from Ocean City, they have not lessened the number of vehicles that move in and out of the city. It is estimated that during the summer 300,000 people cross the bridges each weekend.

SINEPUXENT BAY AND STATE BRIDGE ENTERING OCEAN CITY, MD.

122954

The first bridge built across Sinepuxent Bay was a trestle bridge built by the Wicomico & Pocomoke Railway in 1876.

Cancelled 1930, $11-13

3—Bridge Spanning the Sinepuxent Bay, Ocean City, Md.

U.S. Route 50 begins in Sacramento, California and crosses the continental United States before crossing Sinepuxent Bay and ending at Philadelphia Avenue in Ocean City.

Circa 1950s, $7-9

STATE ROAD BRIDGE APPROACHING OCEAN CITY, MD.

The first automobile bridge to Ocean City was built by the state of Maryland in 1916 and entered the city at Worcester Street.

Circa 1920s, $17-19

Airplane View Showing Bridge Over Synepuxent Bay, Ocean City, Maryland   47

It is estimated that during the summer tourist season, close to 300,000 people cross the U.S. Route 50 and Maryland Route 90 bridges into Ocean City each weekend.

Circa 1940s, $7-9

The drawbridge on U.S. Route 50 raises to let a marlin boat through. The drawbridge causes congested traffic entering and leaving Ocean City during the tourist season.

Circa 1960s, $4-6

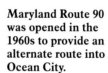

Maryland Route 90 was opened in the 1960s to provide an alternate route into Ocean City.

Circa 1960s, $4-6

Route 90 remains part of U.S. Route 50 until it splits off four miles from Berlin, Maryland. It passes through Ocean Pines, over a bridge to the Isle of Wight, and across Assawoman Bay before reaching Ocean City.

Circa 1960s, $3-5

Visiting Ocean City

Beach Houses, Hotels, and Condominiums

On July 4, 1875, the Atlantic Hotel opened in Ocean City, an event which in many ways marked the beginning of the town. Previously, there had been rooming houses around what would become Ocean City, the earliest of these being Isaac Coffin's Rhode Island Inn, built in 1869. But the Atlantic was fist major hotel here. Four stories tall and with 400 rooms, the Atlantic was called "a marvel in architectural beauty and excellence" and was said to be the equal of any of the East Coast's finest hotels.

A year later, as per the agreement he had made with the Atlantic Hotel Company, Stephen Taber sold fifty acres to the company for the site of a town, the proposed community of Ocean City. This opened the door to a number of developers, investors, and land speculators, many of whom opened hotels and rooming houses of their own. Still others built smaller beach cottages, using them as vacation homes during the summer or as residences in Ocean City year-round.

After World War II ended in 1945, the face of the American hotel began to change. Visitors wanted amenities like air conditioning and television that older hotels in Ocean City were not able to offer. Thus, motels came to Ocean City, the first being the Seascape Motel built in 1954. Most motels did not feature meals that were included with the American plan or the gracious atmosphere associated with the older hotels, but they did have modern conveniences that vacationers were looking for.

The style of accommodations in Ocean City changed again in the 1970s, when a local developer, John Whaley, built High Point, the town's first high-rise condominium. Fifteen stories high, it offered a magnificent view of the beach and the ocean coupled with contemporary design and architecture. Other high rises soon followed, built in the still undeveloped land above 94th Street (what is now "High-Rise Row"), so as not to block the views of existing buildings.

Today, Ocean City is a mixture of many types of accommodations, with summer cottages, motels, hotels, and high-rises often occupying the same block.

Some of the summer cottages built along Baltimore Avenue.

Circa 1920s, $14-16

VIEW OF THE COTTAGES ON BALTIMORE AVENUE, OCEAN CITY, MD.

Cottage Line and Boardwalk Looking North, Ocean City, Md.

12—Cottages and Beach Scene Looking South from Hotel Stephen Decatur, Ocean City, Md.

At the turn of the century, a 25 x 142 foot ocean or bay front lot cost upwards of $25. Today the same property would be worth at least $100,000.

Circa 1920s, $14-16

Beachfront cottages along The Boardwalk.

Circa 1940s, $7-9

THE BELMONT HOTEL AND COTTAGES, OCEAN CITY, MD.

The Belmont Hotel (now the Belmont-Hearne Hotel) was built by Elizabeth Harper Hearne in 1905. It is still run by Elizabeth's descendents and is one of the few hotels in Ocean City that still offers meals and rooms to its guests.

Circa 1920s, $19-21

The Colonial Hotel, one of the many beachfront rooming houses that were built in Ocean City during the early 1900s.

Circa 1910s, $19-21

The Idylwild, Ocean City, Md.

The Idylwild.

Circa 1920s, $19-21

The Mt. Pleasant Hotel opened in 1900 and was located on The Boardwalk between First and North Division Streets.

Cancelled 1918, $19-21

THE PURNELL, OCEAN CITY, MARYLAND

Like many of the hotels and rooming houses in Ocean City, the Purnell featured rooms and efficiency apartments.

Circa 1920s, $14-16

Mayflower and Stephen Decatur-McCabe Apts. and Commander Hotels, Ocean City, Md.

BREAKERS HOTEL, OCEAN CITY, MARYLAND

Starting from the left: the Mayflower Hotel, the Stephen Decatur-McCabe Apartments, and the Commander Hotel.

Cancelled 1947, $7-9

From the back: "BREAKERS HOTEL   Boardwalk and 3rd St.   Eat Well – Sleep Well and Be Served Well."

Circa 1940s, $8-11

The Shoreham Hotel was built by Josephine Richardson Hastings, a businesswoman who was one of the most successful property owners in Ocean City.

Circa 1920s, $17-19

SHOREHAM HOTEL, OCEAN CITY, MD.

The Hamilton.   OCEAN CITY, Md.

Along with the Atlantic and the Plimhimmon, the Hamilton was the center of Ocean City's social life during the summer tourist season.

Cancelled 1913, $17-19

Opened in 1901, the Hamilton was famous for its food, particularly its Sunday specialty of chicken and waffles.

Circa 1910s, $19-21

39—The Colonial on the Boardwalk, Ocean City, Md.

The Colonial was often described as "an outstanding Boardwalk Hotel."

Circa 1940s, $7-9

The Roosevelt Hotel.

$8-10

34—Cavalier Apartments, Ocean City, Md.

Those wishing to be in Ocean City more than a few days often stayed at places like the Cavalier Apartments.

Circa 1940s, $7-9

1B-H2606

OCEAN CITY - HOTEL BISCAYNE.

Hotel Biscayne.

Cancelled 1908, $11-13

Perhaps the most famous feature of the Royalton was its kitchens, where Ethel Kelley could frequently be found cooking from 6:30 in the morning until 10:00 at night.

Cancelled 1931, $9-11

HOTEL ROYALTON, NEW, MODERN, ON THE BOARDWALK, OWNERSHIP MANAGEMENT
OCEAN CITY, MARYLAND

Ethel Kelley and her husband, Harry, purchased the land for the Royalton Hotel for $1,800 in 1925.

Cancelled 1934, $9-11

The Plimhimmon Hotel was also famous for the quality and quantity of its food. For breakfast alone, a guest had his choice of any kind of hot or cold cereal, eggs made to order, kidney stew, lamb chops, bacon, toast, jam, fresh melon, coffee, tea, and a wide variety of juices.

Cancelled 1954, $7-9

Plimhimmon Hotel, Ocean City, Md.

Rosalie Shreve built the Plimhimmon Hotel in 1893. She named the hotel after her family's estate in Talbot County, which, in turn, was named after Plynlimon, the highest point of the Cambrian Mountains in Wales.

Cancelled 1907, $4-6

A unique feature of the Plimhimmon was its own stream-run generator, which produced enough electricity to power the hotel and several of the surrounding cottages as well.

Cancelled 1910s, $19-21

Hotel Plinhimmon, Ocean City, Md.

Half a mile from the beach and The Boardwalk, the Francsic Scott Key Resort advertised a countryclub-like atmosphere away from the crowds and noise of Ocean City proper.

Cancelled 1977, $6-8

After the evening meal, guests at the Atlantic Hotel would often go out for a stroll along the beach or on The Boardwalk.

Circa 1910s, $19-21

The Atlantic Hotel, as seen from The Boardwalk.

Cancelled 1910, $4-6

No. 4034 - Washington Pharmacy, Ocean City, Md.

Atlantic Hotel, Ocean City, Md.

from Edith

Like many of the early hotels in Ocean City, the Atlantic hotel operated on the American plan, offering both meals and rooms to its guests. The largest meal of the day at the Atlantic was the mid-day meal, which was served at noon.

Cancelled 1907, $19-21

According to some early reports, the Atlantic Hotel was built so far above the beach that a team of horses could be driven underneath its porch.

Cancelled 1908, $11-13

Atlantic Hotel, Ocean City, Md.

The Atlantic Hotel, Ocean City, Md.

The Atlantic Hotel was originally owned by the Atlantic Hotel Company until 1892 when it was purchased by the Sinepuxent Beach Company. It was later purchased by Dr. Charles W. Purnell in 1923.

Cancelled 1914, $17-19

Atlantic Hotel, Ocean City, Md.

Dr. Purnell owned the Atlantic Hotel for two years before it burned down in the fire that swept through downtown Ocean City in December 1925.

Cancelled 1907, $19-21

From the back: "You'd meet a girl there, [at the Atlantic] then get together with her again that afternoon on the beach. Then, in the evening, it was back to the Plim or the Atlantic for more dancing. At the Atlantic you had to pay 10 cents a dance to glide around on a dark floor lighted only by reflections from a big, turning ball, suspended from the ceiling and surfaced with hundreds of tiny mirrors."

Circa 1920s, $7-9

ATLANTIC HOTEL AND AUTO LINE • OCEAN CITY, MD.

New Atlantic Hotel, Ocean City, Maryland.

34583

The new Atlantic Hotel rebuilt after the fire in 1925.

(Early Divided Back) $9-11

The Commander Hotel was built in 1931 by Minnie and John B. Lynch, who were former partners of the Royalton's Ethel and Harry Kelley. It opened on Memorial Day 1931 and is still run by members of the Lynch family.

Cancelled 1982, $5-7

Some of the high-rises along "Condominium Row."

Cancelled 1984, $1.50-3.50

Ocean City, Maryland

Photo by Kevin N. Moore

A bird's-eye view of the Quality Inn Boardwalk.

Circa 1970s, $4-6

Quality Inn — Boardwalk

Ocean City, Md.

Many oceanfront hotels, like the Quality Inn Boardwalk, offer umbrella, towel, and beach chair rentals to their guests.

Circa 1970s, $5-7

Another aerial view of the
Quality Inn Boardwalk.

Circa 1960s, $5-7

Swimming pool and tennis courts, as seen from a balcony at the
Best Western Flagship.

Circa 1970s, $5-7

The Atrium inside the Quality Inn was laid out to resemble a tropical garden
complete with tropical plants and exotic birds.

Circa 1970s, $4-6

Seabonay Motel

The Seabonay, located two feet from the beach and one block away from the end of The Boardwalk at 27th Street.

Cancelled 1984, $5-7

Each room at the Surf and Sands Motel had a private porch with a view of the ocean.

Circa 1970s, $5-7

Opened in 1956, the Santa Maria
was one of the first motor hotel
built in Ocean City.

Circa 1980s, $5-7

Milton and Thelma Conner, the son and
daughter-in-law of Willye Ludlam, the
owner of the Santa Maria, purchased the
Dunes Motel in 1966.

Circa 1970s, $5-7

*Windjammer
Apartment - Motel*

**The Windjammer
Apartment Motel.**

Circa 1970s, $5-7

**A view of the Satellite Motel
as seen from the ocean.**

Circa 1980s, $5-7

The Seascape Motel was
built in 1954, the first motel
built in Ocean City.

Circa 1970s, $5-7

Also owned by Ethel Kelley,
the Beach Plaza Hotel was
built in 1953, two blocks
away from the Royalton. It
was purchased by the Phil-
lips family in 1973.

Cancelled 1957, $5-7

Layton Apartments as seen from Sinepuxent Bay.

Circa 1970s, $4-6

The swimming pool at the Harrison Hall Hotel. The hotel itself has been open to guests since 1951.

Circa 1980, $5-7

The Edgewater Motel, which featured twenty-four apartments and cottages.

Circa 1970s, $6-8

**The Cross Roads Motel
located in West Ocean City.**

Circa 1970s, $5-7

**The Sun N' Fun Motel, Baltimore
Avenue at 29th Street.**

Circa 1980s, $5-7

The main office and entrance to
the White Sands Motel.

Circa 1970s, $5-7

The King's Arms Motel.

Circa 1980s, $5-7

The Georgia Belle Motel.

Circa 1980s, $5-7

The Fenwick Inn, a landmark hotel
famous for its rooftop restaurant.

Circa 1980s, $5-7

Restaurants

Before the rise of motels in Ocean City, there were few restaurants. The hotels operated on the American plan, where three meals a day were included in the price of a room, so guests seldom felt the need to venture beyond the hotels for food. Those who weren't staying in a rooming house or hotel purchased food and cooked it themselves or dined at a hotel. Motels built in the 1950s operated along different plans. Those that did have restaurants operated them as separate ventures, not including meals with the price of a room. From the 1950s and beyond, a number of restaurants were built to feed guests who looked beyond their accommodations for meals. In keeping with the atmosphere of a seaside resort, many restaurants served seafood, some of it caught not far from where it was served.

Besides being a restaurant the Ship Café was also a motel and a marina.

Circa 1960s, $5-7

27—Ship Cafe, Ocean City, Md.

9A H2130

The Ship Café was located at 14th Street on the Bay side of Ocean City. It could seat up to 700 people.

Cancelled 1944, $11-13

Reflections Restaurant on 67th Street and Coastal Highway where visitors could "experience the ultimate in fine dining."

Circa 1980s, $2-4

Interior and exterior views of the Samoa Chinese & American Restaurant.

Circa 1960s, $2-4

The Crab Claw, one of Ocean City's many seafood restaurants.

Circa 1970s, $6-8

Excursions

For guests staying in Ocean City, the beach and the Boardwalk were among the activities found in Ocean City. Many visitors took trips to Ocean Downs and Frontier Town, that were close enough for a day-long excursion. Assateague Island (connected to Ocean City until 1933), with its herd of wild ponies and undeveloped beaches, was a popular excursion and camping destination.

Excursionists at R. R. Station, Waiting for Train, Ocean City, Md.

Excursionists wait for the train at the Baltimore, Chesapeake & Atlantic Railway Station. A round trip from Baltimore to Ocean City and back took twelve hours both ways and cost $4.50.

Circa 1920s, $50

Ocean City Golf and Yacht Club in West Ocean City. One of the most popular courses on the East Coast, according to some.

Circa 1970s, $3-5

An aerial view of the track at Ocean Downs. The length of the track is very important in harness racing and often determines the starting and closing speeds of the racers.

$9-11

From the back: "Beautiful Ocean Downs, one of Maryland's modern Harness Racing Tracks. Three miles from Ocean City on Route U.S.50."

Circa 19 $4-6

The Ocean Downs grandstands, capable of seating 15,000 people during racing days.

Circa 1960s, $3-5

Another nighttime view of the Ocean Downs grandstand.

Cancelled 1953, $9-11

The Fort, part of the Western Theme Park at Frontier Town.

Circa 1960s, $8-10

Some of the staff of the Western Theme Park.

Circa 1960s, $8-10

According to legend the wild ponies on Assateague Island are descended from ponies who swam to the island from a Spanish galleon that had shipwrecked off the Maryland coast.

Circa 1970s, $1.50-3.50

The Beach

Even from the town's early days, the beach was what brought visitors to Ocean City, Maryland. Beachcombing, fishing, and swimming are just as popular today as they were in the 1900s.

While activities have largely remained the same over the years, the people on the beach certainly have not. In the 1900s, morning was the time to be on the beach. At noon, beachgoers would retire to their hotels for the midday meal and would spend the afternoon napping or mingling with other guests at the hotel. A fad for tanned skin saw 1920s beachgoers, in Ocean City and around the world, spending more time on the beach, sunbathing well into the afternoon when the sun was its hottest and the chances of getting a suntan were better. From then on, sunbathing joined the list of popular activities on Ocean City's beach.

In 1988 Ocean City embarked on a project to protect and replenish its beaches, which had been steadily migrating westward for several years. They were assisted by the United States Army Corps of Engineers. Phase II of the project began in 1991, when a series of six-foot sand dunes were created along the beach, from 27th Street north to where they meet Delaware's dune chain, at the Maryland-Delaware border. Several additional projects to replenish the beach have been undertaken since then, the most recent in 2006.

A Happy Crowd on the Beach, Ocean City, Md.

A typical happy crowd on the beach.

Cancelled 1926, $14-16

To avoid the afternoon heat, and to avoid missing the big midday meal served at many of the hotels and boarding houses, most vacationers did not stay on the beach past noon.

Circa 1900s, $24-26

Before the invention of sunscreen, beach goers relied on hats, bonnets, and umbrellas to protect them from the sun.

Cancelled 1909, $14-16

The beach was, and still is, one of Ocean City's most popular attractions and was considered an essential part of any excursion to the city.

Cancelled 1910, $24-26

Beach Scene.   Ocean City, Md.

34944

A typical day at the beach.

Circa 1920s, $6-7

Another view of Ocean City's bathing beach.

Circa 1930s, $9-11

BATHING BEACH   OCEAN CITY, MARYLAND

The beach as seen from The Boardwalk.

Circa 1920s, $14-16

Pony riding was a popular beach activity not only in Ocean City, but in many resort towns both in Europe and North America during the early twentieth century.

Cancelled 1908, $4-6

Looking north up the beach from the Pier.

Circa 1910s, $4-6

Surf Bathing.

OCEAN CITY, MD.

Not just for fun and exercise, sea bathing was often done for health reasons as salt water was once thought to have curative and therapeutic properties.

Cancelled 1932, $11-13

To help keep bathers safe when the ventured out into the ocean, ropes were attached to The Boardwalk and to anchors in the ocean giving them something to cling to and prevent them from being pulled under or swept away.

Circa 1930s, $6-8

BOARDWALK AND BEACH FROM OCEAN CITY PIER, OCEAN CITY, MD.

A prize winning entry in Ocean City's annual sand castle building contest.

Circa 1970s, $1.50-3.50

Though it has been around for quite some time, sand sculpting has become popular only in recent years.

Circa 1980s, $3-5

16:—BEACH BOARDWALK AND COTTAGE LINE FROM COAST GUARD STATION, OCEAN CITY, MD.

43906

A picturesque scene showing the beach, The Boardwalk, and Cottage Line.

Circa 1930s, $6-8

View of the beach showing the Castle in the Sand Motel in the background.

Circa 1970s, $5-7

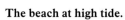

The Beach, Looking North, Ocean City, Md.

The beach at high tide.

Cancelled 1930, $14-16

63

An aerial view of the beach showing The Fishing Pier.

Circa 1970s, $4-6

The sand from Ocean City's beach is said to be some of the finest quality sand in the world.

Cancelled 1975, $4-6

The fishing jetty that marks the end of the beach. Before the 1933 hurricane the beach at Ocean City extended all the way to Assategue Island.

Circa 1970s, $5-7

From the back: "Soft, gentle wave roll up on the beach to the pleasure of vacationers. In the background is The Boardwalk and motels."

Circa 1990s, $2-4

Beach at Ocean City, Maryland   Photo by Richard C. Pullin

The beach, as seen from the Amusement Park.

Circa 1970s, $4-6

THE SURF AND BEACH, BY NIGHT, OCEAN CITY, MD.

17—Boardwalk and Beach Looking North, Ocean City, Md.

3B-H1359

Even at night, the Ocean City beach is crowded.

Circa 1920s, $19-21

Beach goers enjoy the sun, the sand, and the surf.

Cancelled 1957, $7-9

25—Surf Sporting along Ocean Front

Showing the Beach Club, Jackson's Casino, George Washington and Royalton Hotels, Ocean City, Md.

Water skiing began on Lake Pepin in Minnesota, in 1922. It has since spread throughout the world and is a popular water sport in resort communities like Ocean City, Maryland.

Circa 1940s, $7-9

COME ON IN, THE WATER IS FINE.   OCEAN CITY, MD.

By the 1910s more women were learning how to swim making it necessary for manufacturers to use less material in their suits to make swimming easier.

Cancelled 1940, $11-13

Surf Bathing at Ocean City, Md.   42

Surf bathing in the Atlantic Ocean at Ocean City.

Circa 1940s, $4-6

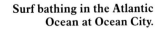

Waves crash against the rocks on the edge of Ocean City.

Circa 1940s, $2.50-4.50

Booming Surf on the Rugged Coast   Ocean City, Md.

70223

The Ocean City Inlet was formed during the hurricane that hit the city in 1933. The city made the inlet permanent in 1935 using funds from both the state and the federal governments to construct a concrete seawall on the the north side.

Circa 1930s, $8-10

THE INLET   OCEAN CITY, MARYLAND

Sand Dunes, on Ocean Highway, between Ocean City, Md. and

Rehoboth Beach. Del.

The Ocean City Beach has been the subject of several beach restoration projects, the most recent of these scheduled to commence after the close of the 2006 tourist season.

Circa 1940s, $13-15

Ocean City, as seen from the salt marshes on the shores of Assawoman Bay.

Circa 1980s, $1.50-3.50

Ocean City, Maryland

The Boardwalk

The Ocean City Boardwalk began as a walkway set up along the beach in 1902. Then, it was known as Atlantic Avenue. It was financed by several oceanfront hotel owners, who built the boardwalk for the convenience or their guests. The original boardwalk was laid out in sections that could be taken up and stored elsewhere overnight.

A permanent boardwalk was built in 1910. It ran five blocks along the beach and was built ten feet above the sand to keep it from washing away. It could be reached from the beach by small inclined walks built along its length. It was customary then for vacationers to spend the evening strolling up and down The Boardwalk after dinner in their best clothes. To appear on The Boardwalk poorly dressed simply would not do. The Boardwalk was extended to 15th Street in the 1920s.

Situated as it was in front of the Atlantic Ocean, The Boardwalk is exposed to storms and has been damaged by them on several occasions. In 1933 and again in 1962, surging waves and wind ripped up huge sections of The Boardwalk and hurled them into the hotels along the beach. After devastation was caused by the 1962 storm, The Boardwalk was rebuilt and extended to its present length, for two-and-a-half miles from South 2nd Street to 27th Street.

The first amusement rides on The Boardwalk were brought to Ocean City in 1887 by Daniel B. Trimper, the owner of the Windsor Resort, a business venture that included two hotels and the amusement center Luna Park. Numerous rides were added to the park (now known as Trimper's Rides) over the years, including outdoor rides. In 1950, a carousel was installed, now being one of the oldest continuously operating carousels in the country.

Another view of The Boardwalk, this one showing the Coast Guard lookout station.

Cancelled 1945, $19-21

Boardwalk showing Coast Guard Lookout, Ocean City, Md.

The southern end of The Boardwalk showing The Boardwalk train station and part of the amusement park.

Circa 1970s, $5-7

1—Boardwalk and Beach from Coast Guard Station at Night, Ocean City, Md.

Looking down The Boardwalk from the Coast Guard station.

Circa 1940s, $7-9

Board Walk showing Atlantic Hotel and Pier, Ocean City, Md.

Along the Boardwalk, Ocean City, Md.

Public transportation on the early Boardwalk took the form of three-wheeled wicker chairs, which could be rented for fifty cents an hour.

Circa 1910s, $19-21

After dinner, many of the well-to-do visitors to Ocean City would spend the evening strolling up and down The Boardwalk. Best clothes were required, it was considered quite unseemly to appear on The Boardwalk in the evening sloppily or poorly dressed.

Cancelled 1918, $24-26

A more modern view of Trimper's Rides & Amusements.

Circa 1980s, $4-6

AMUSEMENT SECTION OF BOARD WALK, OCEAN CITY, MD.

The Amusement section of The Boardwalk was, and still is, home to a fantastic array of rides and games, including Trimper's Carousel, the oldest continuously operating carousel in the United States.

Circa 1920s, $4-6

From the back: "The amusement area at the south end of The Boardwalk near the Inlet is Ocean City, Maryland's first and most complete recreation area."

Circa 1980s, $4-6

GREETINGS FROM OCEAN CITY, MARYLAND

An aerial view of the south end of The Boardwalk showing the Life Saving Station Museum, the Coast Guard Tower and the Trimper's Rides & Amusements.

Circa 1990s, $3-5

18—Boardwalk and Beach Showing Bandstand—Fishing Pier and Recreation Hall, Ocean City, Md.

On their trips up and down visitors and locals would often take a moment to stop at one of the many shops that lined The Boardwalk.

Cancelled 1959, $14-16

Many of the concerts held in the bandstand were given by the Ocean City community band under the direction of Frank Sacca. The bandstand was built in the 1940s by Dr. Francis J. Townsend.

Circa 1950s, $4-6

18—Boardwalk and Beach, showing Fishing Pier and Recreation Hall, Ocean City, Md.

View of The Boardwalk showing the Fishing Pier and the Pier building in the background.

Cancelled 1947, $14-16

30—Boardwalk and Beach North from Roosevelt Hotel, Ocean City, Md.

Rebuilt after a storm in 1962, the Ocean City Boardwalk extends for two and a half miles from S. 2nd Street to 27th Street.

Circa 1940s, $7-9

BOARDWALK NORTH FROM PIER, OCEAN CITY, MD.

1A1674

Strolling along The Boardwalk.

Circa 1920s, $19-21

58 BOARDWALK AND BEACH SCENE, OCEAN CITY, MD.

14 AT 1

The buildup of sand caused by the construction of the jetty on the north side of the inlet in 1935 was so great that the beach eventually became level with The Boardwalk.

Circa 1940s, $7-9

Boardwalk North from Laurel House   Ocean City, Maryland

A view of The Boardwalk and the beach, two of Ocean City's most popular attractions.

Circa 1920s, $17-19

Boardwalk and Beach looking North from The Atlantic Hotel   Ocean City, Maryland

The Boardwalk as seen from the Atlantic Hotel on Boardwalk and Beach looking North from The Atlantic Hotel on Wicomico Street.

Circa 1920s, $11-13

Bicycle riding on The Boardwalk is permitted from 2:00 am to 12:00 pm from May 1 to Memorial Day and from September 1 to September 30. From October 1 to April 30, they are allowed on The Boardwalk any time day or night.

Circa 1960s, $4-6

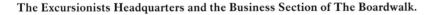

The Excursionists Headquarters and the Business Section of The Boardwalk.

Cancelled 1915, $4-6

From the back: Bicycling on The Boardwalk, Ocean City, Maryland. After a refreshing dip in the surf of the Atlantic Ocean you can enjoy a leisurely ride on The Boardwalk."

Cancelled 1958, $9-11

Having since replaced the old wicker chairs, The Boardwalk Train is now the most popular form of transportation on The Boardwalk.

Cancelled 1967, $5-7

The Boardwalk Trains have two stations one at each end of The Boardwalk.

Circa 1960s, $7-9

No. 212.

Maryland Pharmacy, Ocean City, Md.

The Maryland Pharmacy was owned and operated by Dr. Francis J. Townsend, Ocean City's first medical practitioner.

Circa 1910s, $19-21

The Boardwalk, Ocean City, Md.

Boardwalk, Ocean City, Md.

One of the rooming houses along The Boardwalk, a property that today could cost up to $1 million.

Cancelled 1909, $25

Dr. Townsend owned two other drugstores and soda fountains also located on The Boardwalk.

Circa 1910s, $17-19

Cottages and Boardwalk from the Virginia Cottage, Ocean City, Md.

The Boardwalk as seen from Virginia Cottage.

Circa 1910s, $4-6

BOARD WALK AND OCEAN FROM ATLANTIC HOTEL, OCEAN CITY, MD.

The wicker chairs, shown here, were also a business venture owned by Dr. Townsend.

Circa 1920s, $19-21

31—Boardwalk and Beach and Cottage Line, Ocean City, Md.

A typical crowd on The Boardwalk.

Circa 1930s, $7-9

The Fishing Pier

Near the southern end of The Boardwalk is The Fishing Pier, an Ocean City landmark since its construction in 1907. The pier took three years to build and was financed by a group of local investors called The Ocean City Pier and Improvement Company. At The Boardwalk end of the pier was The Pier Building, which housed a silent movie theater, a dance pavilion, and a poolroom, along with refreshment booths and bowling alleys. Behind The Pier Building, the pier extended over the ocean to another building that housed a roller skating rink. The Fishing Pier was also an excellent place for sport fishing, and equipment could be rented there to visitors who could fish free of charge. It was also the location of annual trapshooting competition held at the beginning of the tourist season.

The original Fishing Pier remained in use from 1907 to 1925, when it was lost to a fire, along with the Atlantic and the Seaside hotels and two blocks of The Boardwalk. In 1929, the Sinepuxent Pier and Improvement Company (organized in June of that year) acquired a new franchise from the city and built a new fishing pier where the old pier had stood. A new Pier Building, with a ballroom on its second floor, was also erected on the site.

Despite its earlier popularity, The Fishing Pier eventually fell into decline by the 1950s. A new pier company, which had taken over The Fishing Pier franchise a few years earlier, proposed to place amusement rides on the pier; the proposal was voted down in 1959. Another attempt to build rides there was made fifteen years later, and it had success. The revitalized Fishing Pier and The Pier Building opened in 1975, under the ownership of a local investor, Charles "Buddy" Jenkins.

In 1979, unusual ice flows caused by cold winter temperatures provided circumstances for 140 feet out of the pier's 700 foot length to be demolished. It was then argued that construction of the stone jetty off the inlet in 1933 had altered water currents along the shore, and that fishing from the pier would not be improved by restoring the pier to its former length. The mayor and town council agreed, and the pier remained at its shortened length. Although it is not used for fishing today, The Fishing Pier stands as one of several landmarks along The Boardwalk.

Ocean City, Maryland, Fishing Pier

Photo by R.C. Pulling

In its early days The Fishing Pier was also known as "Taylor's Ocean Pier" after William Taylor, the president of the Ocean City Pier and Improvement Company.

Circa 1970s, $4-6

View of The Fishing Pier, showing the building at its ocean end, which housed a roller skating rink.

Circa 1910s, $19-21

The Pier Entrance, Ocean City, Md.

By all accounts the Pier was an excellent place to fish, within an hour a fisherman could retire with an excellent catch of trout, spot, kingfish, or hardhead.

Circa 1910s, $24-26

Visitors who did not have time or money to charter a boat could rent equipment and fish from the Pier free of charge.

Circa 1940s, $7-9

Board Walk showing Pier Entrance, Ocean City, Md.

The entrance to the Pier.

Circa 1910s, $30

SIDE VIEW OF THE PIER, OCEAN CITY, MD.

Wishing you a "merry Xmas and a happy Easter, love to mother H.

Will be home sometime soon, next Hand think. (Fan)

PUBLISHED FOR WASHINGTON PHARMACY, OCEAN CITY, MD.

COPYRIGHT, 1907, BY SUDWARTH CO., WASHINGTON, D.C.

The Pier, Ocean City, Md.

The Fishing Pier was also home to another favorite Ocean City pastime trap shooting (competitive shotgun shooting). During the first weeks of the summer season marksmen from all over the East Coast would come to participate in the annual trap shooting competition held at the Pier.

Cancelled 1910, $19-21

The main building of The Fishing Pier, which housed a dance pavilion, and a silent movie theater as well as several billiard tables, bowling alleys, and refreshment stands.

Circa 1910s, $19-21

OCEAN CITY PIER AND BOARDWALK, OCEAN CITY, MD.

Many residents and visitors fondly recall the dances held at the Pier's ballroom and dancing to music played by big band celebrities like Benny Goodman, Glen Miller, Jimmy Dorsey, and Harry James.

Circa 1920s, $4-6

Some of the amusements found on The Pier today.

Circa 1970s, $4-6

Ocean City, Maryland

Photo by Richard Pulling

Out on the Waves

Boats and Fishing

As a seaside resort and "the White Marlin Capital of the World," Ocean City, Maryland, is no stranger to the sports of boating and fishing. Long before a bridge was built across Sinepuxent Bay, boats were the only means of travel between Ocean City and the Delmarva Peninsula. Even after the railroad bridge was constructed in 1876, recreational boating remained a popular activity. Until the creation of the Inlet, most recreational boating was done on Sinepuxent Bay, since there were no places for boats to launch or to anchor safely on the ocean side of the city.

Fishing in the Atlantic Ocean and Sinepuxent Bay was a popular activity during the summer months. The brackish water of the bay was the right habitat for trout and bluefish, while the Atlantic Ocean offered sport fish in deep water and kingfish and trout closer to shore. On any given day, dozens of fishermen could be found lining the shore of the Atlantic Ocean or out on Sinepuxent Bay in rented boats.

The storm of 1933 created the Ocean City Inlet, which led to the growth of recreational boating and fishing within Ocean City. Boats that anchored at Sinepuxent could now reach the Atlantic Ocean, and the rich fishing grounds found within those waters, with no trouble at all.

Big game fishing, which had not been widely pursued before the creation of the Inlet, became popular not long after the Inlet was completed. Two businessmen from Delaware, Jack and Paul Townsend, are credited with breaking the ground, so to speak, with this new sport. In 1934, they came to Ocean City to fish for white marlin, which they suspected could be found in the waters off Maryland's coast. The Townsends found white marlins at the place now known as Jackspot Shoal, but they were unable to catch any. The first white marlin caught was by Captain John Mickle in 1934, an event which is regarded as a high point in the history of sport fishing.

When word of his success spread, sport fishermen descended on Ocean City in droves. The steadily increasing numbers of successful catches led to Ocean City's new nickname, "White Marlin Capital of the World," and to one of the biggest events on the town's social calendar, the White Marlin Open, held each year in August.

Sailing boat at sunset on Sinepuxent Bay.

Circa 1970s, $3-5

Ready For A Sail On The Synepuxent Bay, Ocean City, Md.

Written on the back: "Dearest Pinky: Have been swimming almost every minute since our arrival here. The water is grand + our hotel is right on the ocean. Went sailing in the ocean yesterday + almost got swamped going out. Love, Irene.

Cancelled 1934, $17-19

Synepuxent Bay, Ocean City, Md.

Many of the early pamphlets and advertisements released to promote Ocean City mentioned the excellent opportunities for boating and sailing on Sinepuxent Bay.

Cancelled 1911, $14-16

Sailing on Sinnepuxent Bay, Back of Plimhimmon Hotel, Ocean City, Md.

Sloops sailing on Sinnepuxent Bay.

Cancelled 1911, $9-11

Some of the fish that could be caught off the shores of Ocean City.

Circa 1960s, $3-5

Yacht Basin   Ocean City, Maryland

Modern yachts fall into two classifications sailing yachts, which are powered by sails, and power yachts, which are powered by engines. Both can frequently be seen on the waters around Ocean City.

Circa 1920s, $14-16

13—Harbor Club and Pisces Fishing Boat, Ocean City, Md.

The Pisces, one of many deep-sea fishing boats that made regular fishing tips to the Atlantic Ocean from Ocean City.

Circa 1940s, $9-11

A Youthful Fisherman
Ocean City, Md.

A young fisherman poses with the marlin he has just caught.

Cancelled 1938, $4-6

"ANSWER" AT OCEAN CITY, MD. - NOTED FOR BEST FISHING

From the back: "The 'ANSWER' sails again, leaving Maryland dock at 7.30 A.M. Enjoy our Porgy and Bass fishing, also spinning for Weak fish when practicable. Bring your lunch. Soft drinks and beer aboard. No Whiskey or beer may be brought aboard."

Circa 1940s, $4-6

Fishing boats and docks on Sinepuxent Bay, as seen from underneath the Route 50 bridge.

Cancelled 1969, $6-8

Some of the vessels of Ocean City's famous deep-sea fishing fleet.

Circa 1970s, $5-7

51 FISHING BOATS AT WHARF. OCEAN CITY. MD.

The quality of the fishing at Ocean City attracted a number of notable sportsmen, including President Franklin Delano Roosevelt.

Circa 1940s, $9-11

From the back: "Fisherman's Paradise – a birds-eye-view of one of the many fishing docks."

Circa 1960s, $5-7

One of the largest marlins ever caught off of Ocean City. The first white marlin taken off the Ocean City coast was caught by Captain John Mickle in 1934.

Circa 1970s, $6-8

Fishing from the Inlet. It was the formation of this inlet that lead to Ocean City's prominence as a fishing destination.

Circa 1940s, $5-7

On any given day crowds of fishermen can be found lining both sides of the Route 50 bridge.

Circa 1970s, $4-6

Surfmen and the Coast Guard

Located on the coast of Maryland, the people of Ocean City are not strangers to the hazards posed by the Atlantic Ocean. Storms are not uncommon, and several ships had been wrecked or run aground off Ocean City's shores.

To help imperiled ships and seamen, the United States government established the Life-Saving Service in 1878. Stations staffed by trained Life-Saving Service personnel were established along the Atlantic Coast, particularly in areas with flat beaches exposed to the sea where there were outlying sandbars, few people, and no safe harbors.

The Ocean City Life-Saving Station was established in 1878 on Caroline Street, then at the northern edge of the town. It was staffed by six members of the Life-Saving Service who were overseen by the station's keeper, William T. West. For their work patrolling the beach, keeping watch for storms and shipwrecks, and rescuing ships and sailors in peril on the Atlantic, these men received $20 a month, plus room and board at their station.

In performing a rescue at sea, these surfmen would fire a line from a cannon to the floundering ship, and then secure the line to the beach. Once the line was secure, they used it to bring sailors ashore in a breeches buoy (a canvas seat attached to a ring) or a surf car (an enclosed water-tight capsule), both of which could be pulled along the line. A lifeboat was also kept ready at all times, to take the surfmen to and from a wreck.

In 1890 the United States Treasury authorized the construction of two new lifesaving stations, one on Fenwick Island in Delaware and the other in Ocean City, Maryland. Both were completed a year later. The new station at Ocean City, built on the site of the old station, consisted of a eighteen-by-twenty-foot boat room, the keeper's office, a day room, a kitchen, and a mudroom for storing wet gear on its first floor. On its second floor were the keeper's quarters, the surfmen's bunkroom, rooms for sailors rescued from shipwrecks, and a storage room.

The United States Life-Saving Service operated for forty years along the Atlantic coast until it was merged with the Revenue Cutter Service to form the United States Coast Guard in 1915. In Ocean City, the Coast Guard continued where the Life-Saving Service had been, pursuing the service's duties and operating from its station at Caroline Street until 1964. Then it moved to a new station on Philadelphia Avenue.

Following the relocation of the Coast Guard to Philadelphia Avenue, the abandoned Life-Saving Station was used by several government agencies before finally falling into disrepair. To prevent the station from being demolished in 1977, a group of local citizens formed The Ocean City Museum Society and were able to save the historic building from destruction. The station building was moved from Caroline Street to its present location at the northern end of The Boardwalk, near South 2nd Street. It opened as a museum on December 25, 1978. Since then, the building has continued to operate as a museum specializing in nautical and local history.

The keeper and the surfmen who served at the Ocean City Life-Saving Station. A surfman (a member of a life-saving station's crew) was paid $20 a month plus room and board at whichever post he was stationed.

Cancelled 1910, $4-6

U. S. Life Saving Station, Ocean City, Md.

Originally located on Caroline Street, the Life-Saving Station building was moved to its present location at the edge of the Inlet in 1977. It is the only one of its kind still standing in Maryland.

Cancelled 1907, $4-6

The United States Coast Guard in Ocean City used the old Life-Saving Station as their base of operation from 1915 until 1964 when they moved into their new headquarters on Philadelphia Street.

Circa 1960s, $1.50-3.50

The Coast Guard Tower at the Inlet was erected in 1935. It is the oldest standing watchtower on the Maryland Coast.

Circa 1970s, $5-7

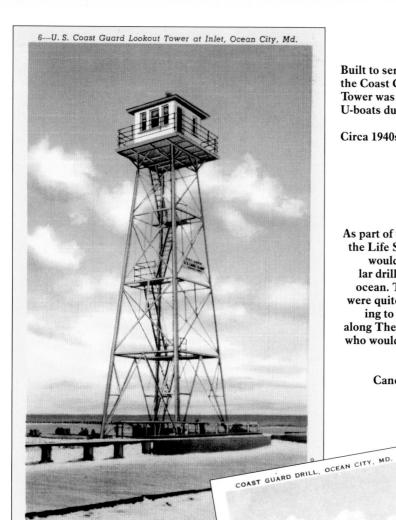

6—U. S. Coast Guard Lookout Tower at Inlet, Ocean City, Md.

Built to serve as a lookout station for the Coast Guard, the Coast Guard Tower was used to watch for German U-boats during World War II.

Circa 1940s, $5-7

Life Saving Crew coming through the Breakers, Ocean City, Md.

As part of their duties the Life Saving crew would hold regular drills out in the ocean. These drills were quite entertaining to the visitors along The Boardwalk who would often stop and watch.

Cancelled 1908, $14-16

COAST GUARD DRILL, OCEAN CITY, MD.

Those rescued by the Life Saving crew, and later the Coast Guard, were often towed to shore in a surf car, an enclosed water-tight capsule, like the one pictured here. The car was attached to a hawser, which allowed it to be pulled back to shore.

Circa 1920s, $11-13

Bibliography

Corddry, Mary. *City on the Sand: Ocean City, Maryland, and the People Who Built It*. Centreville: Tidewater Publishers, 1991.

Hurley, Suzanne B. "Chronicle of Storms Which Influenced Ocean City's History." *Ocean City Life-Saving Station Museum*. http://www.ocmuseum. org/shipwrecks/storms.asp. 9/01/06.

"Ocean City, Maryland." *Wikipedia*. http://en.wikipedia.org/wiki/Ocean_City,_Maryland. 9/01/06.

Stevens, Bob. "A History of the U.S. Life-Saving Service." *Ocean City Life-Saving Station Museum*. http://www.ocmuseum.org/uslss/history1.asp. 9/13/06.

Stevens, Bob. "Museum Building Turns 100 Years Old." *Ocean City Life-Saving Station Museum*. http://www.ocmuseum.org/history2.asp. 9/14/06.

Sullivan, C. John. *Old Ocean City: The Journal and Photographs of Robert Craighead Walker, 1904-1916*. Baltimore: The Johns Hopkins University Press, 2001.

"The Boardwalk History." *Ocean City Boardwalk*. http://www.ocboards.com/history.html. 9/12/06.

"The History of Trimper's Rides & Amusements." *Trimper's Rides & Amusements*. http://www.beach-net.com/trimpers/history/history.html. 9/12/06.

Index